La Diabla

The Wine Cellar Dog

By:

La Diabla

As told to the Ladies of the Club

A Collaborative Effort by The Members Of the Women's
Literary Club of Yuma

Cover and Illustrations by: Steve and Sheli Hudson

authorHOUSE®

AuthorHouse™
1663 Liberty Drive
Bloomington, IN 47403
www.authorhouse.com
Phone: 1-800-839-8640

First published by AuthorHouse   3/24/2011

ISBN: 978-1-4567-5491-4 (e)
ISBN: 978-1-4567-5492-1 (sc)

Library of Congress Control Number: 2011904874

Printed in the United States of America

Any people depicted in stock imagery provided by Thinkstock are models,
and such images are being used for illustrative purposes only.
Certain stock imagery © Thinkstock.

This book is printed on acid-free paper.

Acknowledgements

L a Diabla would like to express a very special thanks to the following friends who helped to make this book possible.

The members of the Women's Literary Club of Yuma for listening to her story and encouraging her to publish her adventure;

Loi Dene Berkey	Mary Emma Berkey
Mary Earle	Ann Farley
Sarah Farley	Marie McGee
Gem Milstead	Sharon Perry
Darla Vannoy	Denise Wah

Nurse Elizabeth and Dr. Margaret for rescuing her and finding her a forever home.

Mike Shelhamer and Sharon Perry for providing her with a forever home, and for hosting a special fundraiser at the Old Town Wine Cellar to help defray the cost of publishing;

Ann Farley for encouraging La Diabla to tell us her story and for coming up with the idea of giving the proceeds to the Humane Society of Yuma to help them ensure that other animals who need to be rescued are given a second chance;

Mary and Fred Earle for also hosting a special wine tasting fundraiser at Yuma's Main Squeeze to help ensure the publication of her book;

Marie McGee and Sharon Perry for taking the time to edit the book and offer ideas to make her story more technically correct and more enjoyable for all readers;

Loi Dene and Mary Emma Berkey for their undying support, encouragement and conviction that it was a story worth telling;

Darla Vannoy for organizing an incredible array of food for the wine tasting fundraisers.

Gem Milstead for putting the words on paper and arranging for a publisher who would publish a story written by a dog;

Steve and Sheli Hudson for the remarkable sketches that help to bring the book to life; and

A special thanks to all those who attended the fundraisers and gave so generously to help her publish her adventure story.

All proceeds go to the Humane Society of Yuma

The Muse

La Diabla the Mutt

CJ The Cockatoo

Sneetch the Labrador

Joe the Labrador

Trent the Retriever

Without their inspiration, encouragement and stimulus there would be no "La Diabla, The Wine Cellar Dog"

La Diabla, CJ, and Sneetch, Lab, & Retriever

The Adventure Begins...

Hi, I'm Diabla, and this is the story of how I came to be known as the "Wine Cellar Dog." It's also the story of how much trouble I can get into without even trying. I've had quite a number of adventures so far, so listen up while I tell you my story.

I was born right here in Yuma, Arizona, somewhere out on the desert; I can't quite remember where exactly. Mom was a Corgi, I think, and Dad was well...a handsome dark furred travelin' man. Anyway, I wandered away from home one sunny afternoon and found myself ambling along next to the canal that runs by Avenue A. It was a hot day, and I got lost because, as usual, I was following my nose and not watching where I was going. I was trying to keep up with this funny little butterfly as it flitted here and there from ground to bush to flower to cactus and I lost track of where I was and where I was going. Well, like I said, it was a really hot day in July and I was getting thirsty and hungry.

That's when I saw two boys running along the canal. They were laughing and throwing sticks and rocks into the water. It looked like they were having lots of fun, so I ran up to join them thinking maybe they'd give me some water and food, and maybe even play with me. Boy oh Boy was that ever a BIG mistake. They weren't nice boys at all, but I didn't know that until it was too late. This is probably the worst and best part of my story. In fact, my whole story as well as my life could have ended right here.

When I grabbed a two-foot long stick that the boys had dropped and ran up to give it to them one of the boys grabbed it and began to tug on it. We played tug o' war for a while until he got mad and let go of the stick.

I was so close to the edge of the canal that when he let go, my feet slipped over the edge and "Splash", I fell into the water. I was really scared. The current was pulling me along so fast I could hardly hold onto the stick. The boys thought it was so funny to see me struggling to stay afloat. I couldn't understand why they wouldn't help me instead of laughing at me. They were throwing rocks into the water just to see them splash next to me. They were cruel, and I was scared.

Then, just when I felt I could not keep my head above water one moment longer, I hit a pile of dirt and branches that had built up along one side of the canal. With my short legs, I struggled to scramble and climb to get to the top of the dirt pile and out of the water. Finally, one of the boys reached down and grabbed the stick I still held in my mouth and pulled me up onto the bank of the canal. Once I got close to the edge, he grabbed me by the scruff of my neck and pulled me out of the water. I thought I was safe now and shook the water off of my coat. But the minute I stopped shaking, one of the boys scooped me up, called me stupid and threw me over a fence into the backyard of a house that backed up to the canal.

It was getting dark, and as I sailed over the fence all I could see was the light coming from the glass doors at the back of the house. I heard the boys run off laughing as they left me to the night.

I landed painfully in a thorny old bougainvillea bush. "Ouch," I whined and cried; every move I made caused me to be poked somewhere with a thorn. When I looked out from the bush I saw two huge dogs, a lab and a retriever named Joe and Trent who were looking out the window. From the noise they made I knew I had caught their attention. They looked really big and pretty hungry to me and I shivered with apprehension. I struggled to get out of the bush to no avail. "Ouch!"

That's when I saw Elizabeth. Of course, I didn't know that was her name at the time, but eventually she became my angel of mercy. Unfortunately, when she opened the glass door just enough to let her dogs out, and to see what they were barking at, they immediately made a rush for the bush where I was stuck. They were barking and snarling and trying very hard to get to me. Luckily, I was just out of reach. Elizabeth came rushing out of the house calling for her neighbors to help her hold back Joe and Trent and get them corralled back in the house. Whew, it was a close call, but Elizabeth and her neighbor managed to get them back inside the house.

After all was quiet, Elizabeth and her neighbor decided that there was something alive in the bush. "Good grief," said Elizabeth, "there's a puppy stuck in that bush." "How in the world did she get up there," said the neighbor? They studied my predicament and then very carefully untangled me from the bougainvillea bush. Elizabeth thanked her neighbor and took me into her house. She had put her dogs out of sight so that I wouldn't be frightened. Then she put me on the counter in her kitchen so she could have a closer look at me. Did I tell you that Elizabeth is a nurse? Well thankfully she is, and she took one look at me and knew just exactly what I needed. She tended to my wounds, gave me food and water, and settled me down in a quiet corner of the kitchen to rest.

I fell asleep listening to Elizabeth on the phone telling her husband, Erin to hurry home to see what their dogs had almost eaten. When he arrived, he looked me over and said, "She looks to be about 4 or 5 months old. She sure can't stay here! We don't know anything about her and our dogs will have her for breakfast." Erin grabbed me up and took me down to his boat shop to spend the night. Actually, I was there for about three days. It was fun, people coming and going, and everyone was so friendly. It was a great place with lots of corners to explore, filled with all kinds of new sights, sounds and smells. I was kept busy greeting everyone and guarding the shop at night.

One day, while I was working at greeting the customers at the boathouse, the nicest lady came in to have the fender on her car fixed at the paint shop. I walked over to greet her and, "whoosh," she scooped me up and cuddled me. It was love at first sight. After Erin told her how I came to be there, Dr. Margaret and Elizabeth got together to find a forever home for me. That's how I came to live with Mike and Sharon. But I had to help the nice lady sell the idea to them. That night, when we went to dinner at Mike and Sharon's house, I was on my best behavior. My coat was all brushed and shiny, and I practiced my most winning smile for my interview with Mike and Sharon.

When we arrived at Mike and Sharon's, I put on my best tail wagging smile, but Sharon looked at me kind of skeptically. Over dinner she listed all the reasons why they couldn't adopt me, i.e., they both worked, they had no doggy door, and there would be no one to play with me all day. I just kept wagging my tail and smiling. I began concentrating on charming Mike; he looked like he could be persuaded to take me in. Finally, Mike said, "Well, maybe I could take her to the shop with me during the day, and she can become my Official Greeter." Yep, it was that easy and that's how I became La Diabla, the Wine Cellar Dog. Everyone smiled now, especially me.

Sharon fixed me up a bed in the spare room, with a blanket and a water bowl, but I wasn't having any of that. I made just enough of a whine to gain her sympathy and she let me sleep with her and Mike.

WOW, this has turned out to be a really great place to live. Mike and Sharon took really good care of me, and even spoiled me a little. I curled up on the bed like a furry little ball and slept peacefully until morning, dreaming of going to work as Official Greeter at the Wine Cellar with Mike. Whatever a "Wine Cellar" was, it sounded like fun.

The next day Mike got ready to go to the Wine Cellar, and just as he promised, I was going to get to go with him. Riding in the car was lots of fun I could see all the other cars and the people in them. Some of the people smiled and waved at me. Seeing the Wine Cellar for the first time was thrilling. What a neat place to play. Mike would throw the ball down the aisles between the rows of wine bottles and I'd run like crazy to catch it and bring it back. Just like at the boat shop, I met lots of nice people. Folks would come in to the Wine Cellar to look over the selection of wines to buy, or just to visit, and of course, I was the Official Greeter. What a great life!

Over the next few months, I met lots of new friends who came to the Shop. Mike and Sharon's friends adopted me too as the Official Greeter. There was Ray, Ann and Sarah; Loi Dene, Greg and Mary Emma; and Gem and Larry. Then there was my favorite attorney, Mike (hopefully I won't ever need an attorney and we can just be friends); and my most favorite, Justice Dave. Like all his friends, I was very sad when he died. I sure miss him. But as time when on my list of friends just grew and grew with Jeff and Marie, Rachel and Sean, and another friend named Mike. I'll bet I have more two-legged friends than any other dog in Yuma.

Because they were my friends, their pets were my friends too. I kind of had a puppy love thing for Ann and Ray's dog, Sneetch, but now we are just friends. I even had a bird as a friend, Gem and Larry's Cockatoo, CJ. He liked girls, so I guess I qualified. He even said "Hello" to me whenever I came to visit. But best of all was living with Mike and Sharon. I got into a little trouble now and then, wandering off through the neighborhood, either at home or over at the Wine Cellar, to see what new sights, sounds, and smells there were to investigate. But, either Mike or Sharon would find me and march me back home, with a stern lecture.

That's how I came to my biggest adventure of all. It was a wine tasting night at the Wine Cellar. All my friends were there, and lots of new people too. I was having a grand time greeting everyone and playing my part as the Official Greeter. I happened to take a particular interest in this one young couple who were enjoying their wine and wandering around the cellar looking at the various items for sale. When they got ready to leave, I escorted them to the back door, and when they opened it and left, I scooted out behind them to walk them to their car.

It was such a lovely evening I decided to wander down to the river. I strolled along Maiden Lane to the corner of First Street.

There were other folks and their dogs walking over to Gateway Park, so I followed them across First Street to the park entrance. When I got to the river, I saw one fellow with a grocery cart sitting under the trees, enjoying the evening breeze. He looked pretty lonely, so I decided that maybe he would enjoy having a friend sit with him. Soooo, I just sauntered on over and plopped down beside him. He looked at me and said, "Well, aren't you a pretty girl," and began to pet my coat and scratch my ears. The night was pretty cool, but snuggled up against his leg, I was nice and warm and began to get drowsy. Soon I fell fast asleep. I didn't know that by this time, all my friends at the Wine Cellar were out searching for me.

When I woke up, I had a rope leash tied to my collar and the stranger was getting ready to leave Gateway Park. The stranger said, "Come along now, we've a long way to walk to get to Quartzsite. I want to get to the Yuma Proving Ground by this evening to find a good place to camp for the night." Oops, I really just wanted to go home, but I didn't know how to tell the man. My collar had my owner's name and phone number on it, but I guess he didn't know how to read. Oh well, I guess I'd just have to stay with the stranger 'til I figured out how to get home. Boy oh Boy, Mike and Sharon would really be mad at me this time for wandering away this far. I guess I'd be getting more than a lecture when I got home, if I got home.

As we sat by the river, the stranger shared some snacks with me and let me drink water out of the river. Then we were up and moving down Gila Street turning left on Giss Parkway to make our way toward Highway 95. I was really beginning to miss Mike and Sharon now. I cried a little as we passed within sight of the Wine Cellar's back door, but the Stranger just shushed me up and kept walking.

When I faltered, the stranger put me in the grocery cart, and we continued down Giss Parkway. We turned right at what was once LA Yuma Freightline and, being careful to avoid traffic, finally made our way to Highway 95. We passed the Highway 95 Café and kept on moving toward the Yuma Proving Ground.

For the next few months, the stranger and I wandered all the way up to Quartzsite where we spent the winter among lots of snowbirds who come here every winter to avoid the cold snowy weather back home. It took us a long time to get up to Quartzsite, and I was really tired by the time we got there.

Along the way, we ran into a coyote mother and her cubs near their den. The stranger and I watched her puppies play. I wanted to run over and say Hi and play with the puppies too, but the stranger wouldn't let me. He said the mother would probably kill me and feed me to her puppies. Yuck, that didn't sound so good, so I just watched them play from a safe distance.

Out by the Yuma Proving Ground, we came upon a herd of burros. I ran over to get a closer look, but they just snorted and kicked up their heels at me. I ran through the herd nipping at their heels and causing them to scatter in all directions. It was fun, but the stranger called to me to come back. He said we had to find a place to spend the night before it got dark. We always had to make sure that our campsites under an ironwood tree had no snakes, scorpions, or tarantulas living there. We'd gather rocks and make a campfire, eat our dinner, and usually fall asleep early. We still had a long way to go so we usually started our walks very early in the morning, sometimes even before the sun came up.

One afternoon as we walked along the desert, we surprised a Gila monster. Even though I was up in the grocery cart, it really scared me. It even scared the stranger who chased it away with a broom. It's a really big and mean looking poisonous lizard. I've heard that they're pretty shy and are rarely seen on this side of the state. Actually, from the safety of the cart, it was kind of interesting looking. It had a stubby tail, like it stopped growing too soon, and funny looking pink stripes and splotches on a black body. At almost two feet long, it was dangerous. I saw on a nature program that Mike and I watched one night that although they were very shy, they were also known to attack almost anything seen as a threat. I was sure glad when it scampered away and that we were going in a different direction.

I woke up one morning and looked up to see this big, beautiful bighorn sheep standing on the ridge above our campsite. He was a truly majestic ram with the sun rising behind his big curling horns. He stood with his head held high and looked out over the desert like a king gazing out over his realm. Once he was satisfied that all was well, and that we weren't a threat to his kingdom, he turned and ambled away toward the watering hole located on the Colorado River. Then the stranger woke up and started fixing breakfast. While we ate, I kept looking up at the ridge hoping that the bighorn sheep would return so the stranger could see it too.

There were thousands of people in Quartzsite in trailers and fifth wheels and buses. There were so many different accents from folks visiting from the Midwest, the Northwest, the East Coast, and even from Canada. Everyone was really friendly and gave me snacks whenever I visited. It was kind of a fun winter, but I was getting really homesick. However, when May came, the snowbirds started to leave and Quartzsite became almost like a ghost town. I started to get lonely for home and wished we would go back to Yuma and find Mike and Sharon. I began to whine with sadness in my sleep, missing home.

The next morning, the stranger looked at me and said, "Well, little girl, I guess it's time we headed south again before it gets too hot."

My ears perked up at the idea of going home. I just knew that if I could get back to Gateway Park in Yuma, I could find my way back to the Wine Cellar. I would have to stick with the stranger until we got to Yuma and then find a way to escape from my rope leash. I cheered up and the thought of going home. Off we went, back down Highway 95 toward Yuma. We passed all the places we had used as campsites. I didn't see the bighorn sheep again, but I saw coyotes, roadrunners, burros, and lots of lizards. Thank goodness we didn't run into a Gila monster again; once was enough! We even saw some jackrabbits hopping across the desert, and now and then a rattler slithering across the road. By the time we reached Yuma, it was getting pretty hot and I was tired of traveling.

It had been more than a year since I had started my adventure with the stranger, and I was worried that Mike and Sharon and all my friends had forgotten me.

When we walked down Gila Street toward Gateway Park, I looked longingly across the parking lot to the back door of the Wine Cellar. I just couldn't pass it up, so I began to bark and whine and pull on my rope leash to get away from the stranger. He'd been good to me, fed me well, but he was still a stranger. It's kind of funny now that I think about it, I never did hear anyone call him by his name, and he never called me anything but "Little Girl."

At last the stranger stopped and gave me a long sad look. He turned and stared across the parking lot and let out a big sigh.

Finally the stranger said, "Well, little girl, I guess that shop is your home, huh? I think I always knew that, but I was lonely and I just wanted a friend to travel with me. I can tell you've been sad for quite a while now. Okay, let's see if anyone is there to let you in." We walked across Gila Street and the parking lot, and stood looking at the back door of the Wine Cellar. At last we crossed Maiden Lane and walked up the steps to the back door of the shop. The stranger gave my ears a scratch and said, "This is where I leave you Little Girl. Thanks for spending time with me. I hope your family will take you back. You're fatter than when we met, but I think they'll recognize you." Then he untied my rope leash, patted me on the head again, and opened the door just enough for me to nose my way in.

I stood for just a moment taking in the familiar sights and sounds of the Wine Cellar. I heard Mike humming and the familiar sound of tinkling bottles as he worked. My heart was beating so fast as I walked down the aisle between the bottles. I was scared that Mike wouldn't remember me or be so angry he would just toss me out the back door. I stopped and looked up to see Mike standing by the counter. He had stopped humming and, as I trotted up the aisle he turned and stared at me like I was a mirage. In his mind's eye, he must have seen me like this many times since I disappeared. When he realized I was real, he ran forward and scooped me up in a big bear hug. I licked his face and hands and wiggled and wagged my tail and we celebrated my homecoming. I think there were tears in both our eyes.

We decided to surprise Sharon, so we didn't tell her I was coming home with Mike. Boy, this was the best ride I'd had in a long time. There we were, driving along listening to the radio. Mike kept giving me a pat on the head and a hug. He still could hardly believe I was really home. When we got home, I trotted through the front door of the house, and then scooted out to the back yard though my doggie door. Soon, Sharon came out of the home office and caught sight of something moving in the backyard. When she came outside to investigate, she stood there stunned for a moment. She called "Diabla?" and I came running. She scooped me up and hugged and petted me and we celebrated with happy tears all over again. She looked at me and said "Boy you stink, and you're fat. It's a bath and a diet for you little devil."

Yep, that's my name, La Diabla, Spanish for The She Devil. It was so good to be home again! I had really missed all the sights, smells, and sounds of home while on my adventure. Mostly, I missed the love of my family and friends. I still have a tendency to follow my nose, but Mike and Sharon keep a close eye on me and work to keep my wanderlust under control. And, of course, when I went back to the Wine Cellar all my friends celebrated my homecoming.

Well, that's my adventure. I hope you enjoyed my story, and hope I'll see you around Yuma.

LOCAL YUMA POOCH TELLS OF HER AMAZING ADVENTURE

La Diabla, rescued by a local businessman and his wife, finds a loving home and fulfilling career as hostess of the Old Town Wine Cellar. This is the story of how she wandered away from the Wine Cellar one evening during a wine tasting event. Suffering from a case of Followshernoseitis she gets lost and spends the next 13 months traveling with a homeless gentleman.

He takes her under his wing, feeding and caring for her while they traveled across the desert to Quartzsite. Read how she meets and greets the fascinating animals who roam the desert, the various snowbirds who frequent the desert in the winter, and eventually finds her way home.